Seven Secrets to Sales Success in the Age of AI

Written By: Ryan J. Morse

Catalyst Sales Solutions Group LLC.

Copyright © 2024 Ryan Joseph Morse
Catalyst Sales Solutions Group LLC.
All rights reserved.
ISBN: 9798324539139

DEDICATION

To the salespeople tired of chasing leads and hungry for a winning strategy in the digital age, this book equips you with the tools to outmaneuver change, leverage AI, and close more deals. To my incredible family and the dedicated team at Catalyst Sales Solutions Group LLC, whose unwavering support fueled this journey. Thank you.

Introduction

The sales landscape is undergoing a seismic shift. Artificial intelligence (AI) is no longer science fiction; it's here, and it's transforming the way we sell. But fear not, AI isn't here to replace you – it's here to **empower you**.

This book equips you with the knowledge and strategies you need to thrive as a human salesperson in the age of artificial intelligence.

Each short chapter is packed with actionable insights, delivered in clear and concise language that will guide you through the exciting world of AI in sales, showing you how to leverage its capabilities to become a more efficient, effective, and ultimately, successful salesperson.

Chapter 1: Become a Partner, Not a Competitor: Unleashing the Power of AI in Sales

Let's face it, AI can be a bit intimidating. But here's the good news: the current state of AI in sales is designed to **complement your skills, not compete with them.**

AI excels at automating tedious tasks like data analysis, lead nurturing, and even basic prospecting.

This frees you to focus on what humans do best –

- Building relationships
- Understanding customer needs
- Closing deals.

Your AI Arsenal: Tools for Success

AI offers a diverse toolbox specifically designed to make your life easier. Here are some key tools and their applications in the sales process:

- **Prospecting:**

    Imagine having a tireless assistant constantly scouring the web for qualified leads. AI-powered prospecting tools can analyze vast amounts of data to identify potential customers who perfectly match your ideal buyer profile.

- **Lead Scoring:**

    Qualifying leads used to be a time-consuming process. AI can analyze customer behavior, demographics, and online interactions to assign a score to each lead, indicating their likelihood to convert. This allows you to prioritize your efforts and focus on the most promising leads.

- **Customer Relationship Management (CRM):**

    AI-powered CRMs are taking traditional systems to the next level. These intelligent tools can automatically log interactions, predict customer needs, and even suggest relevant follow-up actions.

Building the Dream Team: Humans and AI Working Together

Here's the first key to maximizing your success: **view AI as your partner, not your competitor**.

Leverage AI's ability to crunch data and identify patterns. Use its insights to **personalize your sales approach** with targeted messaging and a deeper understanding of customer needs.

Imagine this: an AI system provides you with a detailed profile of a potential customer, highlighting their interests and purchase history.

Armed with this knowledge, you can tailor your pitch, anticipate potential objections, and ultimately, craft a more compelling offer.

You've gone from a generic salesperson to a trusted advisor, and that's the power of the human-AI partnership.

By embracing AI, you'll gain valuable time, improve your efficiency, and achieve superior sales performance.

For now, remember – AI is here to help you win, not replace you. Embrace the change, become a partner with AI, and watch your sales soar!

Chapter 2: Decode the Customer Brain: Understanding AI-powered Consumer Behavior

The days of the static buyer persona are over. Today's customer journey is a dynamic dance influenced by a silent partner – artificial intelligence (AI). This chapter will equip you to understand how AI shapes customer behavior, empowering you to personalize your sales approach and build trust in an age of automation.

Welcome to the Age of the Algorithmic Customer
AI is woven into the fabric of our lives, silently influencing everything from product recommendations to search results. Customers are bombarded with information, and AI plays a significant role in how they research, evaluate, and ultimately decide on purchases.

Here's how AI shapes the customer brain:

- **Personalized Experiences:** AI algorithms track customer behavior, preferences, and online interactions. This data is used to create targeted advertising, suggest relevant products, and essentially curate a personalized shopping experience for each customer.

- **Social Proof on Steroids:** Recommendation engines powered by AI leverage "social proof" to a whole new level. Imagine a customer researching a new laptop. AI, having analyzed their browsing history and online reviews, might highlight positive reviews from people with similar interests, significantly influencing their decision.

Decoding the Data: Tailoring Your Approach

The good news? This wealth of AI-derived data is a goldmine for salespeople. Here's how to leverage it:

- **Ditch the Generic Pitch:** Gone are the days of one-size-fits-all sales pitches. Use AI insights to tailor your messaging to each customer's specific needs and interests. This personalized approach fosters a sense of genuine connection and builds trust.

- **Predict Before They Ask:** AI customer behavior analysis can help you anticipate customer concerns and objections. By addressing these proactively, you demonstrate your understanding of their needs and establish yourself as a trusted advisor.

Building Trust in the Digital Age: The Human Touch

AI is powerful, but it can't replace the human element of sales. Building trust and emotional connections is still paramount. Here's how to strike the right balance:

- **Empathy is King:** AI can't replicate genuine empathy. Actively listen to customer concerns, understand their unique situations, and demonstrate a sincere desire to help. This builds trust and fosters long-term relationships.

Remember: Your role is no longer simply "selling" a product. You're a trusted advisor, a guide navigating customers through a complex, AI-influenced decision-making process. By embracing AI insights and remaining true to the human element of sales, you'll build trust, connect with your audience, and ultimately achieve sales success.

Chapter 3: The Power of Storytelling: Crafting Compelling Narratives in an AI-driven World

In the age of automation and AI-powered sales tools, one human ability remains irreplaceable: the **power of storytelling**. This chapter equips you to master this art form, differentiating yourself from AI and forging emotional connections with your audience. Learn how to craft impactful narratives that resonate with customer needs, identified through the lens of AI insights.

Why Storytelling Matters More Than Ever
AI excels at data analysis and personalization. It can churn out targeted messages and product recommendations. But AI can't replicate the human ability to tell a compelling story. Here's why storytelling remains crucial in the age of AI:

- **Emotional Connection:** Stories tap into human emotions, creating a deeper connection with your audience. Facts and figures tell, but stories **make people feel**. By evoking emotions, you make your product or service more memorable and increase the likelihood of purchase.

- **Building Trust:** Sharing narratives allows you to showcase your company's values, mission, and the positive impact it has on customers. This transparency builds trust and fosters long-term relationships.

- **Humanizing Your Brand:** AI can feel impersonal. Storytelling injects a human element into your sales approach, making your brand relatable and fostering a sense of connection.

Crafting Compelling Narratives: Your Storytelling Toolkit

Now that we understand the "why," let's delve into the "how." Here are key techniques for crafting compelling sales narratives:

- **The Hero's Journey:** This classic story structure resonates across cultures. Position your customer as the hero on a journey, and your product or service as the tool that helps them overcome challenges and achieve their goals.

- **Problem-Solution-Transformation:** Identify the problems your customers face, showcase how your product provides a solution, and paint a picture of the positive transformation they can experience.

- **Data with a Human Touch:** AI provides valuable customer data. Integrate this data into your stories, but remember, data points alone are cold. Weave them into a narrative that resonates emotionally.

Leveraging AI for Storytelling Impact

AI can be your silent storytelling partner. Here's how to leverage AI insights to tailor your narratives for maximum impact:

- **Identify Customer Needs:** AI customer behavior analysis can reveal common pain points and aspirations. Use this knowledge to craft narratives that directly address customer needs and resonate with their desires.

- **Personalize Your Stories:** AI can segment your audience based on demographics and online behavior. Tailor your stories to each segment, using specific examples and challenges that resonate with that particular group.

- **Track and Analyze:** Use AI tools to track customer engagement with your stories. These data insights allow you to refine your narratives and maximize their impact.

By mastering the art of storytelling and leveraging AI insights, you'll craft narratives that differentiate you from AI-powered tools. You'll build emotional connections, earn trust, and ultimately close more deals.

Chapter 4: Mastering the Art of Negotiation: Humanizing the Deal in an AI Age

The age of AI has brought innovation to the sales process, with tools that generate contracts and automate proposals. While AI can crunch numbers and draft documents, the human touch remains essential in securing deals. This chapter equips you with the negotiation skills needed to navigate the complexities of human interaction, build trust, and achieve win-win solutions in the age of AI.

Why Human Negotiation Still Matters

AI can certainly generate contract templates. However, successful negotiation goes beyond just the numbers. Here's why human interaction remains paramount:

- **Understanding Needs, Not Just Numbers:** AI struggles to understand the nuanced needs and motivations behind a client's stance. Your role as a skilled negotiator is to actively listen, uncover underlying concerns, and tailor your approach accordingly.

- **Building Rapport:** AI can't build trust and rapport, the cornerstones of strong business relationships. Through effective communication, empathy, and a genuine desire to find common ground, you can establish a positive negotiation environment that fosters trust and collaboration.

- **Navigating Challenging Conversations:** AI can't handle the unexpected roadblocks that often arise during negotiations. Your ability to think on your feet, address objections creatively, and find solutions that benefit both parties becomes crucial in securing the deal.

Honing Your Negotiation Skills for the AI Age

Now, let's sharpen your negotiation toolkit. Here are key strategies for success:

- **Active Listening:** This is more than simply hearing words. Pay attention to your client's tone, body language, and unspoken cues to truly understand their needs and concerns.

- **Mirroring and Matching:** Subtly mirroring your client's communication style (tone, pace, word choice) fosters a sense of connection and builds rapport.

- **Open-Ended Questions:** These encourage your client to elaborate on their needs and pain points, providing valuable insights that can guide your negotiation strategy.

Strategies for Win-Win Solutions

The goal is not to win at all costs, but to create a situation where both parties feel they've achieved a valuable outcome. Here's how to achieve win-win solutions:

- **Focus on Value, Not Just Price:** Shift the conversation from pure price negotiation to highlighting the long-term value your product or service brings to your client's business.

- **Identify Common Ground:** Look for areas where your interests and your client's interests overlap. This common ground can be the foundation for a mutually beneficial agreement.

- **Creative Problem-Solving:** Don't be afraid to think outside the box. Explore alternative solutions or find ways to structure a deal that addresses your client's specific concerns.

Building Long-Term Relationships in Negotiation

A successful negotiation shouldn't be the end of your relationship with a client - it should be the beginning. Here's how to use negotiation to build long-term partnerships:

- **Focus on Collaboration, Not Competition:** Always view your client as a partner.

- **Deliver Value Beyond the Deal:** Go the extra mile to ensure your client receives excellent post-sale support and feels like you're genuinely invested in their success.

- **Maintain Open Communication:** Foster an environment of open communication with your client, where concerns can be addressed promptly and a foundation of trust is established.

By mastering these human-centric negotiation skills, you'll navigate the AI age with confidence, building trust with your clients, securing win-win deals, and fostering long-term, successful partnerships.

Chapter 5: Embrace Disruption: Adapting Your Sales Mindset for the Future

The sales landscape is a constant dance of change. New technologies emerge, customer expectations evolve, and the very nature of what it means to be a salesperson continuously shifts. This chapter equips you with the tools to navigate this dynamic environment, fostering a growth mindset that allows you to thrive in the face of disruption and transform change into opportunity.

The Growth Mindset: Your Key to Adaptability

The foundation of success in the ever-evolving world of sales lies in cultivating a **growth mindset**. This mindset is based on the belief that your abilities are not fixed but can be developed and expanded through continuous learning and effort. Here's why a growth mindset is crucial:

- **Embraces Challenges:** Those with a growth mindset view challenges as opportunities to learn and grow. They don't shy away from difficult sales situations, but see them as stepping stones to improvement.

- **Resilience in the Face of Setbacks:** Everyone faces setbacks in sales. A growth mindset fosters resilience, allowing you to bounce back from rejection and learn from mistakes.

- **Lifelong Learning:** The growth mindset embraces the idea that learning is a lifelong journey. It encourages continuous exploration of new sales techniques, technologies, and industry trends.

Strategies for Lifelong Learning and Skill Development

So, you're committed to continuous learning. Now, how do you put that into action? Here are key strategies:

- **Become a Knowledge Sponge:** Read industry publications, attend conferences and workshops, and actively seek out mentors and coaches. Embrace online learning platforms and podcasts to expand your knowledge base.

- **Practice Makes Perfect:** Don't just learn – actively apply your newfound knowledge and skills. Role-play sales scenarios, practice your presentation skills, and test out new techniques with low-risk opportunities.

- **Embrace Feedback:** Feedback is a gift, even when it's critical. Actively seek feedback from colleagues, mentors, and even clients. Use it to identify areas for improvement and refine your sales approach.

Turning Disruption into Opportunity: Embrace Change

Change can be daunting, but within disruption lies immense opportunity. Here's how to reframe your perspective and turn disruption into a competitive advantage:

- **Be a Trend Spotter:** Actively seek out emerging technologies and trends in sales. By understanding what's coming, you can anticipate shifts in customer behavior and adapt your approach accordingly.

- **Embrace New Tools:** AI and other technologies are transforming the sales landscape. Don't fear these tools – learn how to leverage them to your advantage.

- **Be an Early Adopter:** Be the first in your network to embrace innovative sales tools and techniques. This positions you as a thought leader and attracts clients seeking a forward-thinking sales partner.

Developing Strategies for Specific Disruptions

Let's delve deeper into specific disruptive forces and strategies to navigate them:

- **The Rise of E-commerce:** Customers are increasingly tech-savvy and comfortable buying online. Develop an omnichannel sales strategy that seamlessly blends online and offline interactions.

- **Shifting Customer Expectations:** Today's customers expect personalized experiences. Embrace AI and data analytics to understand your customer needs on a deeper level and tailor your approach accordingly.

- **The Gig Economy:** The traditional sales force is evolving. Adapt to a more flexible model, utilizing freelancers and contractors to supplement your sales team when needed.

Remember, change is inevitable. By adopting a growth mindset, embracing lifelong learning, and viewing disruption as an opportunity, you'll transform yourself into a future-proof salesperson, ready to conquer any challenge the evolving sales landscape throws your way.

Chapter 6: Building Your Personal Brand: The Human Advantage in the Age of AI

In a world increasingly dominated by AI-powered tools and automation, one thing remains irreplaceable: **you**. Your unique skills, experience, and personality are your greatest assets.
This chapter equips you with the strategies to build a powerful personal brand – the human advantage in the age of AI.

Why Personal Branding Matters More Than Ever

AI can churn out data-driven content and generate personalized marketing messages. But it can't replicate the trust and connection fostered by a well-developed personal brand. Here's why building your brand is crucial:

- **Differentiate Yourself:** A strong personal brand sets you apart from the sea of generic salespeople. It showcases your unique value proposition and attracts clients seeking a genuine human connection.

- **Build Trust and Credibility:** In a world saturated with marketing messages, people crave authenticity. A personal brand built on genuine expertise and transparency fosters trust and credibility, making you a more compelling salesperson.

- **Become a Thought Leader:** Sharing your knowledge and insights through your personal brand positions you as an expert in your field. This attracts potential clients and establishes you as a trusted advisor.

Leveraging Your Unique Strengths

Your personal brand isn't about creating a fake persona. It's about amplifying your strengths and showcasing what makes you exceptional. Here's how to identify your unique selling proposition (USP):

- **Strengths and Passions:** What are you naturally good at? What excites you in your sales career? These strengths and passions become the foundation of your personal brand.

- **Experience and Expertise:** Years of experience and accrued knowledge are invaluable assets. Highlight your specific expertise and how it benefits your clients.

- **Communication Style:** Are you a data-driven analyst or a charismatic storyteller? Identifying your communication style helps you connect with the right audience.

Building Your Online Presence: Your Stage in the Digital Age

The internet is your personal brand's stage. Here are strategies for establishing a strong online presence:

- **Craft a Compelling Website:** Your website is your digital storefront. Showcase your expertise, highlight your successes, and make it easy for potential clients to connect with you.

- **Embrace Social Media:** LinkedIn, Twitter, and industry-specific platforms are valuable tools for sharing your insights, engaging with potential clients, and building your network.

- **Content is King:** Create high-quality content that showcases your expertise. Write blog posts, develop e-books, or share insightful videos to establish yourself as a thought leader.

Developing Your Thought Leadership Position

Thought leadership isn't about self-promotion; it's about sharing valuable knowledge and insights that benefit your audience. Here's how to cultivate a thought leader mindset:

- **Identify Industry Pain Points:** What are the key challenges your clients face? Focus on creating content that addresses these pain points and offers relevant solutions.

- **Engage in Industry Discussions:** Participate in online forums, speak at conferences, and contribute to industry publications. This positions you as an expert and increases your visibility.

- **Be Authentic and Consistent:** Share your unique perspective and insights. Authenticity builds trust and fosters a loyal following.

Actionable Strategies for Building Your Brand Every Day

Building a personal brand is an ongoing process. Here are actionable strategies to integrate into your daily routine:

- **Network Actively:** Connect with potential clients and industry figures at conferences, online events, and through social media. Build genuine relationships, not just transactional connections.

- **Offer Value Beyond the Sale:** Become a trusted advisor to your clients, not just a salesperson. Offer ongoing support, share industry updates, and demonstrate genuine interest in their success.

- **Track Your Progress:** Use analytics tools to track the reach and engagement of your online content. Refine your strategies and identify areas for improvement based on data insights.

By leveraging your unique strengths, fostering genuine connections online, and establishing yourself as a thought leader, you'll build a powerful personal brand that sets you apart in the age of AI. This human advantage makes you the trusted advisor your clients seek, propelling you towards continued sales success.

Chapter 7: The Future of Sales: Humans and AI Working Together

The future of sales is a collaborative dance between human expertise and artificial intelligence. As we discussed, AI brings automation and data analysis, but the human touch remains irreplaceable. This final chapter emphasizes the strategies we discussed to thrive in this evolving landscape, exploring the skills needed for future success and actionable steps to position yourself as a leader in the AI-powered sales revolution.

A Glimpse into the Future: Collaboration, Not Competition

The future of sales isn't about AI replacing humans. It's about **humans and AI working together** as a powerful force. Here's what the future holds:

- **AI-powered Automation:** Imagine AI handling repetitive tasks like data entry, lead qualification, and scheduling appointments. This frees up your time to focus on high-value activities like building relationships, closing deals, and providing strategic guidance to your clients.

- **Hyper-personalized Selling:** AI will analyze vast amounts of customer data to personalize your sales approach at an unprecedented level. Imagine crafting targeted messages, addressing specific customer needs, and predicting buying behavior – all powered by AI insights.

- **The Rise of the Customer-Centric Salesperson:** In a world saturated with AI-powered recommendations, the human salesperson who prioritizes customer needs and builds genuine connections will be invaluable.

The Skills and Qualities of the Future Salesperson

While AI automates tasks, it can't replicate the human element of sales. Here are the key qualities and skills in demand for future success:

- **Strategic Thinking and Problem-Solving:** AI excels at data analysis, but strategic thinking remains a human strength. Identify complex customer challenges and craft innovative solutions that leverage both AI insights and your own creativity.

- **Emotional Intelligence and Relationship Building:** Building trust and rapport are crucial for fostering long-term client relationships. Hone your emotional intelligence to understand customer needs, demonstrate empathy, and cultivate genuine connections.

- **Data Literacy and Analytical Skills:** While AI crunches numbers, understanding data allows you to interpret its insights. Learn to leverage data to inform your sales strategy, identify trends, and make data-driven decisions.

- **Adaptability and Continuous Learning:** The sales landscape is in constant flux. Cultivate a growth mindset and a commitment to lifelong learning. Be ready to embrace new technologies, refine your skills, and adapt to changing customer needs.

Positioning Yourself for Success: 5 Actionable Steps for the Future

The future of sales is bright for those who embrace the AI revolution. Here are actionable steps you can take right now to position yourself for success:

- **Upskill Yourself:** Invest in training programs that develop your data literacy, analytical skills, and knowledge of AI-powered sales tools.

- **Embrace New Technologies:** Don't fear AI; explore it! Learn how to leverage AI tools to streamline your workflow, gain valuable customer insights, and personalize your sales approach.

- **Network with AI Experts:** Connect with individuals who are at the forefront of AI in sales. Learn from their experiences and stay ahead of the curve.

- **Become a Thought Leader:** Share your knowledge and insights about the future of sales and the human-AI partnership. Position yourself as an expert in this evolving landscape.

- **Focus on Building Strong Customer Relationships:** While AI automates, personal connections remain paramount. Focus on building trust, providing value beyond the sale, and becoming a trusted advisor to your clients.

By developing the right skillset, embracing continuous learning, and fostering strong customer relationships, you'll position yourself as an indispensable asset in the future of sales. The human-AI partnership will redefine the industry, and those who embrace this collaboration will be the true leaders in the years to come.

www.ingramcontent.com/pod-product-compliance
Lightning Source LLC
Chambersburg PA
CBHW050251230526
45470CB00005B/2214